# 101 iD€A$ for CONT€MPORAR¥ ARTi$T$

(((Alejandro Saint-Barthélemy)))

I0492527

# [[[000]]]

*El verdadero vanguardista es inaceptable,*
*imposible de admirar e ilegible.*
(César Aira)

*Ser vanguardista es no aceptar que lo bueno es bueno y*
*lo malo es malo, e inventarse una nueva definición de*
*lo bueno y lo malo.*
(César Aira)

*It is only an auctioneer who can equally and*
*impartially admire all schools of art.*
(Oscar Wilde)

*Be the worst you can be:*
*life's too long for patience and virtue.*
(Charles Saatchi)

*If a man never contradicts himself, the reason must be*
*that he virtually never says anything at all.*
(Erwin Schrödinger)

*Efectivamente, nada ha envejecido jamás más deprisa y*
*de peor manera que lo que en un momento dado*
*calificaron de «moderno».*
(Salvador Dalí)

# [[[00]]]

*I quote others only in order to better express myself.*
(Michel de Montaigne)

*The love of luxury is rooted in the depths of a man's ♥.*
(Nietzsche)

*Tyranny is the deliberate removal of nuance.*
(Albert Maysles)

*Art is not what you see, but what you make others see.*
(Edgar Degas)

*Without contraries there is no progression. Attraction
and repulsion, reason and energy, love and hate...*
(William Blake)

*When you change the way you look at things, the things
you look at change.*
(Max Planck)

*Be less curious about people
and more curious about ideas.*
(Marie Curie)

*Those who can make you believe absurdities,
can make you commit atrocities.*
(Voltaire)

# [[[0]]]

## <u>MOSCA</u>

Modern
Original
Shocking:
Contemporary
Art.

Mechanism to create art.
Democratization of fine arts.
The end of psychological misery, style, talent, genius...

It's not what you know but who you know.
It's not the product you have but how well you sell it.

Read César Aira's essay *Sobre el arte contemporáneo*.

Create a majestic title for the artwork, if needed.
Tracey Emin's bed didn't need it.
Damien Hirst's stuffed shark did need it indeed.
Create an awesome explanation for the artwork.
Every interpretation is genuine and legitimate.

Do something simple &/or too personal and explain it
in a way nobody will understand it but you, if so.
(☞□□□)☞☜(°ㄅ°☜)

## STICKERS

Canvas with sticker/stickers on them.
Canvas covered in painting (*horror vacui*)
but where the sticker goes,
or even where the sticker goes.
Play with this idea.
*I'm sticking with you 'cause I'm made out of blue…* ♫♪
♪ ┌( · o·)┘ ♪ └( ·o·) ┐

## Art Attack

(1) Put a coin on a canvas.
(2) Cover the canvas with a blue Hawaiian cocktail
or Hawaiian blue acrylic painting mixed with water,
splashing the chosen material over the canvas
with a brush, giving the effect of somewhat rain.
(3) Put a sticker of a penguin with an umbrella
in the white space made by the coin.

*… et voilà !*

["Hey, I could have done that, bro," Average Joe said.
"But you didn't do it, did you?" I said, full of myself.]

## SWIMMING POOLS

Different installations
depending on the season, market, et cetera.
Play with this idea.
*Salarymen drink my spine…* ♪♪
♪ ┌( • o•)┘ ♪ └ ( •o•) ┐

### Art Attack
(1) *Beer swimming pool*: liquid gold + semen.
(2) *Blue wine swimming pool.*
(3) *Coca-Cola® swimming pool.*
(4) *Olympic-size swimming pool
covered in gummy bears instead of water*:
people must enter the pool naked,
wearing a bikini or a speedo,
and swim, have sex and/or eat.

*… et voilà !*

## DOLPHIN

Everybody loves dolphins.
Remember that a cute puppy (*Puppy*)
covered with flowers
in a gigantic size (43 ft)
is a Koon's Kitsch masterpiece.
Remember Damien's stuffed shark too.
Play with this idea.
*I'll come back again as a dolphined dolphin...* ♪♪
♪ ┌( · o·)┘ ♪ └( ·o·) ┐

## Art Attack

Dolphin, spouting water from its mouth, made of SSS:
Sapphires  + Silver + Sugar.

*… et voilà !*

# [[[004]]]

## <u>CONDOM</u>

A condom full of confetti
hanging from a unicorn's
corny horn
made of corn
(corn syrup is sweeter than sugar).
Fast cummers love condoms.
Everybody likes confetti.
Everybody loves unicorns.
Some people like corn.
Everybody loves sex.
Play with this idea.
*The loveliest of all animals is the unicorn...* ♪♪
♪ ┌( · o·)┘ ♪ └ ( ·o·) ┐

## <u>Art Attack</u>

(1) Fill a condom with confetti.
(2) Break a unicorn's horn.
(3) Put a corn where the unicorn's horn used to be.

*… et voilà !*

# [[[005]]]

## SANDWICH

A starfish with seaweed
between two beautiful
woman's hands,
being the one on top covered in caramel and icing.
Play with this idea.
*Eating her fingers like just another meal...* ♪♪
♪ ⌐( · o·)⌐ ♪ └ ( ·o·) ¬

## Art Attack

(1) A starfish.
(2) Laminaria as lettuce.
(3) Honey and liquid poo, stirred, as caramel.
(4) Cocaine as sugar.

*... et voilà !*

**[[[006]]]**

## <u>TUELJE</u>

Tupac Shakur
Elvis Presley
Jesus Christ
holding hands.

Newest
hottest
hippest
artwork in years.

Play with this idea.
*All eyez on me… ♪♪*
♪ ┌( • o•)┘ ♪ └( •o•) ¬

### <u>Art Attack</u>

(1) A sculpture of 2Pac.
(2) A sculpture of the King.
(3) A sculpture of the Messiah.

*… et voilà !*

# [[[007]]]

## GODOT

Installation.
Notes of every currency in the world
coming out of the ventilation system.
Play with this idea.
*Godot has come to save you...* ♪♪
♪ ┌( · o·)┘ ♪ └( ·o·) ┐


## Art Attack

(1) A room.
(2) A gallery.
(3) People.
(4) Notes of every currency in the world.
(5) Ventilation system.

*… et voilà !*

## NAPOLEON COMPLEX

A turtle eating a crocodile.
Play with this idea.
*My love is bigger than your love...* ♪♪
♪ ┏( ˙ o˙)┛ ♪ ┗ ( ˙o˙ ) ┓

## Art Attack

(1) A stuffed giant turtle.
(2) A stuffed baby crocodile.

*… et voilà !*

# [[[009]]]

## **UNTITLED**

Two hands,
one open with a free discount ticket
and another one close, empty.
Most people would choose the closed one.
Mystery sells.
Play with this idea.
*So show me yours and I'll show you mine...* ♪♪
♪ ┌( · o·)┘ ♪ └ ( ·o·) ┐

## **Art Attack**

(1) A stuffed closed hand.
(2) A stuffed open hand.
(3) A discount ticket.

*... et voilà !*

# [[[010]]]

## TRUE LOVE

A stuffed human heart
covered in chocolate.
Play with this idea.
*If I was your vampire...* ♪♪
♪ ┌( • o•)┘ ♪ └( •o•) ¬

## Art Attack

(1) Stuffed heart.
(2)  Chocolate made of poo.

*... et voilà !*

## <u>BIKINI SINS</u>

Bikinis made of heavy materials
&
painted in attractive colours.
Feminist message.
Play with this idea.
*Take this pink ribbon off my eyes...* ♪♪
♪ ┌( · o·)┘ ♪ └ ( ·o·) ┐

## <u>Art Attack</u>

(1) Bikinis made of heavy materials.
(2)  Loud paintings.
(3) Flashy paintings.
(4) Garish paintings.

*… et voilà !*

# [[[012]]]

## PATRIARCH

A Madrilenian *porra* with
stuffed testicles attached to it.
Feminist message.
Play with this idea.
*Sex… is… violent…* ♪♪
♪ ┌( • o•)┘ ♪ └ ( •o•) ┐

## Art Attack

(1) A Madrilenian porra.
(2) Stuffed testicles.

… *et voilà !*

## POINT-BLANK

Gorgeous stuffed lower woman's body
attached to a huge doughnut
working as the upper part.
Feminist message.
Play with this idea.
*Because you're so sweet you lift up "my heart"…* ♪♪
♪ ┌( · o· )┘ ♪ └( ·o· )┐


## Art Attack

(1)  Gorgeous stuffed lower woman's body.
(2) Huge doughnut.
(3) 3 different models:
A) Wearing sexy knickers.
B) Naked, with a sexy vagina.
C) Naked, without a vagina.

*… et voilà !*

# [[[014]]]

## POLITICAL CORRECTNESS

A transparent crutch painted in skin colour
with milk on the inside symbolizing the bones.
Artwork made by an alien who was told about art but
never seen any.
Play with this idea.
*Are we human… or are we dancers…?* ♪♪
♪ ┌( • o•)┘ ♪ └ ( •o•) ┐

## Art Attack

(1) A crutch.
(2) Semen, milk and other white fluids.
(3) Necessary chemicals to make it work.
(4)  Skin colour.

*… et voilà !*

# [[[015]]]

## LIVE & DIE

*The way we die, the way we live:*
*Expecting to finally start living.*
(Alexander Akyna)


A broken straw in a half-empty/half-full glass.
Why not? Anything goes.
Artwork which grows out of the title,
as in Hirts's *A Thousand Years*,
or its created after a majestic artwork,
as in Hirst's
*The Physical Impossibility of Death*
*in the Mind of Someone Living*
for his pickled shark.
Play with this idea.
*Live & die by the beach with ya bitch...* ♪♪
♪ ⌐( · o·)⌐ ♪ └ ( ·o·) ¬


### Art Attack
(1) A broken straw.
(2) A half-empty/half-full glass.

*... et voilà !*

**[[[016]]]**

# A WORKING CLASS HERO
# IS SOMETHING TO BE...

Marxist message.
Decadent bourgeoise.
Two golden statues on a bed inside a bank
(John and Yoko's *Bed-in for Peace* at a Hilton Hotel)
with two placards
(*Herd Peace* and *Meh Peace*):
The male statue dressed as an artsy hippy,
the female statue dressed with a fur coat.
Play with this idea.
*All we are saying... is give porn a chance...* ♪♪
♪ ┌( · o·)┘ ♪ └( ·o·) ┐

## Art Attack
(1) A bed.
(2) Two golden statues.
(3) Clothes.
(4) Placards.
(5) Bubblegum pink.
(6) Thick brush.
(7) A bank.

*... et voilà !*

## <u>TEMPVS FVGIT</u>

A golden watch
close to eight small boxes of sugary cereals.
Play with this idea.
*It was only yesterday life was a touch more sweet...* ♪♪
♪ ┌( ˙ o˙)┘ ♪ └( ˙o˙) ┐

### <u>Art Attack</u>
(1)  Golden watch.
(2) Eight small boxes of colourful cereals.

*… et voilà !*

## AN APPLE A DAY

An Apple keyboard made of teeth.
Post-surrealist object.
Go back to the surrealists to find inspiring and plausible
explanations to the weirdest connections
(check out Salvador Dalí on his
*La persistencia de la memoria*
[Camembert, space and time, Jesus's flesh...).
Play with this idea.
*Apple for Apple... tooth for tooth...* ♪♪
♪ ┌( ･ o･)┘ ♪ └ ( ･o･) ┐

### Art Attack
(1) Apple keyboard.
(2) Teeth.

*... et voilà !*

## POST-DUCHAMP READYMADES

*My work is always a readymande.*
(Ai Wei Wei)


Most contemporary art is a regurgitation of Marcel's.
Duchamp broke with all the past, with all the traditions,
and you can't found a school with a bust at the entrance
of an artist who set all artistic traditions on fire,
but that's exactly what has happened,
as well as with the most known religions in the world.


Most contemporary art are readymades
with better titles,
more appealing objects (or more gross)
and bigger sizes than Duchamp's ones.


An example of a Neo-Post-Duchamp readymade:
*In Advance of Rotten Arm.*
A nod to Rrose Sélavy in the very title,
but with a more appealing object than her spade:
clitoris on a camera tripod in order to fuck it
without the need of moving the arm.
Play with this idea.


*Tu coño es mi droga… Tu coño es mi droga…* ♪♪

## <u>MARILYN</u>

Marilyn Monroe by Andy Warhol
reinterpreted by Mr. Brainwash
and now re-reinterpreted by you
by putting a retro/vintage/hipster
Duchampian *La Gioconda*'s moustache on it.

Play with this idea.

*That's how it goes... Anything goes...* ♫♪

♪ ⌐( ˙ o˙)⌐ ♪ ∟( ˙o˙ )¬
♪ ⌐( ˙ o˙)⌐ ♪ ∟( ˙o˙ )¬
♪ ⌐( ˙ o˙)⌐ ♪ ∟( ˙o˙ )¬
♪ ⌐( ˙ o˙)⌐ ♪ ∟( ˙o˙ )¬
♪ ⌐( ˙ o˙)⌐ ♪ ∟( ˙o˙ )¬
♪ ⌐( ˙ o˙)⌐ ♪ ∟( ˙o˙ )¬
♪ ⌐( ˙ o˙)⌐ ♪ ∟( ˙o˙ )¬
♪ ⌐( ˙ o˙)⌐ ♪ ∟( ˙o˙ )¬
♪ ⌐( ˙ o˙)⌐ ♪ ∟( ˙o˙ )¬
♪ ⌐( ˙ o˙)⌐ ♪ ∟( ˙o˙ )¬
♪ ⌐( ˙ o˙)⌐ ♪ ∟( ˙o˙ )¬
♪ ⌐( ˙ o˙)⌐ ♪ ∟( ˙o˙ )¬
♪ ⌐( ˙ o˙)⌐ ♪ ∟( ˙o˙ )¬
♪ ⌐( ˙ o˙)⌐ ♪ ∟( ˙o˙ )¬
♪ ⌐( ˙ o˙)⌐ ♪ ∟( ˙o˙ )¬
♪ ⌐( ˙ o˙)⌐ ♪ ∟( ˙o˙ )¬

## NYLIRAM

Marilyn Monroe by Andy Warhol
reinterpreted by Mr. Brainwash
and now re-reinterpreted by you
by putting her upside down.

Play with this idea.

*You can love her... and love me at the same time...* ♫

♪ ┌( ˙ o ˙)┘ ♪ └( ˙o˙ )┐
♪ ┌( ˙ o ˙)┘ ♪ └( ˙o˙ )┐
♪ ┌( ˙ o ˙)┘ ♪ └( ˙o˙ )┐
♪ ┌( ˙ o ˙)┘ ♪ └( ˙o˙ )┐
♪ ┌( ˙ o ˙)┘ ♪ └( ˙o˙ )┐
♪ ┌( ˙ o ˙)┘ ♪ └( ˙o˙ )┐
♪ ┌( ˙ o ˙)┘ ♪ └( ˙o˙ )┐
♪ ┌( ˙ o ˙)┘ ♪ └( ˙o˙ )┐
♪ ┌( ˙ o ˙)┘ ♪ └( ˙o˙ )┐
♪ ┌( ˙ o ˙)┘ ♪ └( ˙o˙ )┐
♪ ┌( ˙ o ˙)┘ ♪ └( ˙o˙ )┐
♪ ┌( ˙ o ˙)┘ ♪ └( ˙o˙ )┐
♪ ┌( ˙ o ˙)┘ ♪ └( ˙o˙ )┐
♪ ┌( ˙ o ˙)┘ ♪ └( ˙o˙ )┐
♪ ┌( ˙ o ˙)┘ ♪ └( ˙o˙ )┐
♪ ┌( ˙ o ˙)┘ ♪ └( ˙o˙ )┐
♪ ┌( ˙ o ˙)┘ ♪ └( ˙o˙ )┐

# [[[022]]]

## MARILYN MANSON

Marilyn Manson by Mr. Brainwash, reinterpreted by showing it as an X-ray portrait.

Play with this idea.

*It's all anatomic as the size of your pito… ♪♪*

♪ ┌( · o·)┘ ♪ └( ·o· )┐
♪ ┌( · o·)┘ ♪ └( ·o· )┐
♪ ┌( · o·)┘ ♪ └( ·o· )┐
♪ ┌( · o·)┘ ♪ └( ·o· )┐
♪ ┌( · o·)┘ ♪ └( ·o· )┐
♪ ┌( · o·)┘ ♪ └( ·o· )┐
♪ ┌( · o·)┘ ♪ └( ·o· )┐
♪ ┌( · o·)┘ ♪ └( ·o· )┐
♪ ┌( · o·)┘ ♪ └( ·o· )┐
♪ ┌( · o·)┘ ♪ └( ·o· )┐
♪ ┌( · o·)┘ ♪ └( ·o· )┐
♪ ┌( · o·)┘ ♪ └( ·o· )┐
♪ ┌( · o·)┘ ♪ └( ·o· )┐
♪ ┌( · o·)┘ ♪ └( ·o· )┐
♪ ┌( · o·)┘ ♪ └( ·o· )┐
♪ ┌( · o·)┘ ♪ └( ·o· )┐
♪ ┌( · o·)┘ ♪ └( ·o· )┐
♪ ┌( · o·)┘ ♪ └( ·o· )┐
♪ ┌( · o·)┘ ♪ └( ·o· )┐

# [[[023]]]

## SPIT PAINTINGS

Spit on canvases
after having drunk different juices
with different colorings on them.
In the tradition of Damien's spot paintings.

Political message.
Criticism of the food industry.

It's not the product you have but how you sell it, they
say...

Play with this idea.

*Spit on a stranger... You are a bitter stranger...* ♪♪
♪ ⌐( · o·)⌐ ♪ └( ·o·)¬
♪ ⌐( · o·)⌐ ♪ └( ·o·)¬
♪ ⌐( · o·)⌐ ♪ └( ·o·)¬
♪ ⌐( · o·)⌐ ♪ └( ·o·)¬
♪ ⌐( · o·)⌐ ♪ └( ·o·)¬
♪ ⌐( · o·)⌐ ♪ └( ·o·)¬
♪ ⌐( · o·)⌐ ♪ └( ·o·)¬
♪ ⌐( · o·)⌐ ♪ └( ·o·)¬
♪ ⌐( · o·)⌐ ♪ └( ·o·)¬
♪ ⌐( · o·)⌐ ♪ └( ·o·)¬
♪ ⌐( · o·)⌐ ♪ └( ·o·)¬

## <u>CHAMPS NEVER DIE</u>

Henri Ford's sculpture (cryopreserved)
with a halo and a briefcase packed with Benjamins.

*Making money is art
and working is art
and good business is the best art.*
(Andy W.)

Making money is the ultimate American talent.

Making money is the rarest talent there is.

Never feel ashamed for being a bad artist
but a good entrepeneur.

Play with this idea.

*Stars in our own car... We can drive away...* ♫♪
♪ ⌐( ˙ o˙)⌐ ♪ ∟( ˙o˙ ) ¬
♪ ⌐( ˙ o˙)⌐ ♪ ∟( ˙o˙ ) ¬
♪ ⌐( ˙ o˙)⌐ ♪ ∟( ˙o˙ ) ¬
♪ ⌐( ˙ o˙)⌐ ♪ ∟( ˙o˙ ) ¬
♪ ⌐( ˙ o˙)⌐ ♪ ∟( ˙o˙ ) ¬
♪ ⌐( ˙ o˙)⌐ ♪ ∟( ˙o˙ ) ¬
♪ ⌐( ˙ o˙)⌐ ♪ ∟( ˙o˙ ) ¬

## GREED IS GOD

*Everybody wants to win the lottery*
*I want to win the lottery, everybody*
*You want to win all the lotteries everyday*
*The rest is sex.*
(Alexander Akyna)

Something related to excrements.
A big statue of poo was sold for 2 million dollars, so…

Everybody is greedy.
Everybody knows about God,
the ultimate celebrity in the air, ether
or in the flesh of Jesus.
$450.3 million for Leonardo's masterpiece
*Salvator mundi.*

Every critic knows about alchemy,
Freud, Dalí,
the relationship between dung and gold...
Just create something.
Why not?
Anything goes.

Act, then think, or don't think at all
and just remember some key words

to throw like sedative darts:
alchemy, Freud, Dalí, Manzoni...
You can go a step beyond and call the artwork
*Dunggoldgreedgod*, end of story.

*Nihil sine Deo.*

Play with this idea.

*This is not a love song... This is not a love song...* ♪♪
♪ ┌( • o•)┘ ♪ └ ( •o•) ┐

# HITLER

Maurizio Cattelan 's statue of him (*Him*)
was sold for $17.2 million.

Hitler is amongst the best known celebrities
of the 20th century,
and it's exploited like that in good and bad books,
good and bad movies,
contemporary art…

People don't pay a lot of attention to the other dictators
(Franco who? Idi what?),
so I recommend sticking to Hit.

An installation of Adolf realizing what a bad artist
and/or "no future" artist he was
while working on a canvas in a men's hostel
seems juicy enough to me.

Play with this idea.

*Another nazi attack… A skinhead is cracked…* ♪♪
♪ ┌( ˙o˙)┘ ♪ └( ˙o˙)┐
♪ ┌( ˙o˙)┘ ♪ └( ˙o˙)┐
♪ ┌( ˙o˙)┘ ♪ └( ˙o˙)┐

## <u>DON'T TRY</u>

If anything signed by a contemporary artist will be sold
by a decent amount of money,
I don't know why you would have to struggle at all,
and I'm not talking about skill or old rules of art
(craft, depth and beauty)
but contemporary ones (MOS).

We are evolutionary conditioned
to follow the easiest path
due to our species being the only one
aware of their limited lifetime expectancy,
so it's only natural that Hirst himself
ended up "making" ("thinking") spot paintings...

*I just wanted to find out where the boundaries were.*
*So far I've found there aren't any.*
*I just wanted to be stopped,*
*and no one will stop me.*
(St. Damien the Apostole).

Do whatever you want.
Anything goes.

*Here we are now… Entertain us!…* ♫♪
♪ ┌( • o•)┘ ♪ └ ( •o•) ¬

# [[[028]]]

## <u>DIET TIP</u>

Cute (in size) installation.
*The one and only diet tip you'll ever need.*
Instant noodles with tofu, multivitamin and green tea.

Play with this idea.

*We eat animals… and aliens will drink us…* ♪♪

♪ ┌( · o·)┘ ♪ └( ·o· )┐
♪ ┌( · o·)┘ ♪ └( ·o· )┐
♪ ┌( · o·)┘ ♪ └( ·o· )┐
♪ ┌( · o·)┘ ♪ └( ·o· )┐
♪ ┌( · o·)┘ ♪ └( ·o· )┐
♪ ┌( · o·)┘ ♪ └( ·o· )┐
♪ ┌( · o·)┘ ♪ └( ·o· )┐
♪ ┌( · o·)┘ ♪ └( ·o· )┐
♪ ┌( · o·)┘ ♪ └( ·o· )┐
♪ ┌( · o·)┘ ♪ └( ·o· )┐
♪ ┌( · o·)┘ ♪ └( ·o· )┐
♪ ┌( · o·)┘ ♪ └( ·o· )┐
♪ ┌( · o·)┘ ♪ └( ·o· )┐
♪ ┌( · o·)┘ ♪ └( ·o· )┐
♪ ┌( · o·)┘ ♪ └( ·o· )┐
♪ ┌( · o·)┘ ♪ └( ·o· )┐
♪ ┌( · o·)┘ ♪ └( ·o· )┐
♪ ┌( · o·)┘ ♪ └( ·o· )┐

# [[[029]]]

卐卐卐

Nazism is far from being old-fashioned
(maybe more shocking in previous decades,
but what the hell shock us nowadays, anyway).

Jake & Dinos Chapman.
Recycle J&D idea of the nazi sculptures fucking,
by making it even more shocking:
A woman with penis fucking a man with a pussy,
one black,
one Asian,
one muslim,
one jew,
and so on.

Be concerned with the boundaries
of what society is willing to tolerate
and overpass any one of them.

*Today, no one is scandalized; society has found ways to
nullify the provocative potential of a work of art,
adopting before it an attitude of consumerist pleasure.*
(André Breton)

*With vice... I hold the mic device...* ♪♪

## FRAMED REALITY

*Hirt's pickled shark is rotting and needs to be replaced.*
*Should it still be worth £6.5m?,*
asked The Daily Telegraph back in 2006.

This is how you'd have answered that back in the day:
*Y€$, and even more millions.*
*I personally and professionally estimate double.*
*Not as awe as it used to be,*
*now we find it more down to earth.*
*New meanings arise.*
*The artwork grows with us over time,*
*but*
*the impossibility of death in the mind of someone living*
*persists*
*no matter how close we are to our last breath,*
*while time itself keeps on consuming*
*our sense of reality, self and our very skin cells.*
*We are all in the gutter,*
*but some of us think of our dead souls*
*swimming amongst the stars,*
*like Damien did,*
*in the shape of a tiger shark.*

*Am I lying to you when I say that I believe in you...?* ♪♪
('ー`)y-~~

## <u>PLAY IT AGAIN AND AGAIN, SAM</u>

*Art cannot be criticized because every mistake is
a new creation.*
(Mr. Brainwash).

Robert Hughes once said,
*Being a critic is like being a piano-player
in a whorehouse;
you don't have any control over the action
going on upstairs.*

The best defense is a good offense:
*An educated person's ideas of Art
are drawn naturally from what Art has been,
whereas the new work of art is beautiful by being
what Art has never been...
A temperament capable of receiving,
through an imaginative medium,
and under imaginative conditions,
new and beautiful impressions,
is the only temperament
that can appreciate a work of art.*
(Oscar Wilde)

*Don't pay any attention to what they write about you.
Just measure it in inches.* (Drella)

（ ^_^ ） o 自自 o （ ^_^ ）

## STUCKISM

So these Stuckists, Remodernists, want you dead.
Their artistic impetus is forward and radical.
Or so they say.
They are all about art with spiritual value.
Conceptualism requires brains, after all.
*Anti-Anti art*, or so they claim.

*Spiritual Renaissance now,* in the days of Instagram!
They do sound like Don Quixote to me.

We agree that *there is nowhere else for art to go.*
That's why we stopped and now only pose, gov'nas.
Music, films, fashion and video games are our best art.

Unlike Stuckist defensive, reactionary,
fated to defeat doomed position,
we embrace our times,
like any good artist of the past did.

The best art movement of the last decades is
the art market itself.
It doesn't get any more absurd than that.
We aren't able to create masterpieces again, though.

After centuries of art, artists, public, dealers, etc.,

we have become terribly lucid, hence Postmodernists.

Postmodernists see clearly that art cannot longer be,
in a world where our gods are celebrities
(they walk on water, yes, but only when you freeze it)
and afterlife a TV series,
a lot more than a self-help pill,
mating strategy,
adult's toy
or way of making a living,
burn out or fade away.
Is ReMo art willing to prevent that, but not able?
Then it is impotent;
is ReMo art neither able not actually willing,
in their predilection for amateurism,
to prevent that?
Then why so serious, Sir Artist?

*Remodernism in general embraces*
*the bravery of the amateur,*
*so craft is a strange thing to think about.*
*Craft is usually about something striving for perfection,*
*without flaws, to be "professional".*
The cult of the amateur is a Postmodernist trait,
Jesse Richards, get your head out of your ass.
*No temas la perfección —nunca la alcanzarás.*
Wise words from Salvador Dalí,
a man who had the dexterity of an old master,

so don't fear it, ReMos,
and ask a little bit more of yourselves.
Japanese concept of *Wabi-sabi*
sounds to me, in your case,
like a Postmodernist excuse
for laziness more than the sign of genius
or a New Renaissance, "Remodernists".


Neglecting craftsmanship, Remodernists or Stuckists
make themselves look worst than us,
contemporary artists,
since, at least,
we deny craftsmanship in order to focus on the mental,
whereas they avoid it without adding anything else.
Let me quote the so very quotable Oscar Wilde again:
*Ours has been the first movement*
*which has brought the handicraftsman and the artist*
*together,*
*for remember that by separating the one from the other*
*you do ruin to both;*
*you rob the one of all spiritual motive*
*and all imaginative joy,*
*you isolate the other from all real technical perfection.*
*The two greatest schools of art in the world,*
*the sculptor at Athens*
*and the school of painting at Venice,*
*had their origin entirely in a long succession of simple*
*and earnest handicraftsmen.*

*It was the Greek potter who taught the sculptor that*
*restraining influence of design which was the glory of*
*the Parthenon;*
*it was the Italian decorator of chests and household*
*goods who kept Venetian painting always true to its*
*primary pictorial condition of noble colour.*
*For we should remember that all the arts are fine arts*
*and all the arts decorative arts.*
*The greatest triumph of Italian painting was the*
*decoration of a pope's chapel in Rome*
*and the wall of a room in Venice.*
*Michelangelo wrought the one,*
*and Tintoretto, the dyer's son, the other.*
*And the little 'Dutch landscape,*
*which you put over your sideboard today,*
*and between the windows tomorrow,*
*is' no less a glorious 'piece of work than the extents of*
*field and forest with which Benozzo has made green*
*and beautiful the once melancholy arcade of the Campo*
*Santo at Pisa,'*
*as Ruskin says.*

*No te empeñes en ser moderno.*
*Por desgracia, hagas lo que hagas,*
*es la única cosa que no podrás evitar ser,*
famously said reactionary,
highly craftsman turned into modern artist
Salvador Dalí.
Think about it.

See ReMo artworks and conclude that they are not
moving nor crafted nor deep nor beautiful nor soulful
nor naturally elegant Wabi-sabi (Hiroshige),
nor even horrible…
Lukewarm or mediocre "at best",
oh, the oxymoron! —food for bin.
That *emotion* and *experience* they write about
in their manifestos…
nowhere to be seen,
unless you consider a skeleton crying
(Philip Absolon, *Breakdown*)
a purge of the artist's heart in a kool Wabi-sabi,
highly personal and/or highly innovative manner…
and not a flyer from a hipster lo-fi acoustic concert
in a posh café on Notting Hill, that is.
*Authenticity, self-expression and autonomy*, they claim.
Any 6-year-old artist embodies that, & without tryin'.
*Artists who don't paint aren't artists*,
"The Stuckist Manifesto" claims;
*Artists who paint vapidly and badly should suffer art…*
*arthritis,* we answer back.

Stuckists or Remodernists are not cynical, ironical
nor nihilist…
which doesn't mean that their art is not as bloodless
as Postmodernist one,
yet lacking the intellectualism of some of the latter.

Another so-very-lucid Stuckist claim is

*Art that has to be in a gallery to be art isn't art.*
*That*'s exactly what Duchamp found out to not be true!
The artist can matter more than the artwork.
We love Van Gogh because we know about him,
for his flowers would not be the same flowers
if they had been painted by some random person.

I guess Stuckists must love this quote by Hockney:
*Don't listen to what an artist say, but see what he does;*
*that's what counts.*
Then again, since Duchamp's intellectual revolution,
conceptual art,
that quote sounds like coming from a dinosaur
and not an artist.


<(((">


><>


<*)))-{


><(((*>

<(((">

# [[[033]]]

## <u>STELLA VINE</u>

Stuckist converted into Unstuckist.

She was indeed truly discovered by Charles...
Saatchi, not Thomson, after all.

Her Before Charles artworks, nonexistent.

Cartoonish images of celebrities
with a shocking message attached to 'em,
what she's known for,
what she likes doing,
her finest art:
MOS,
contemporary art.

Richard Dorment of *The Daily Telegraph*
praised Vine's work in a show for its ability to
*skewer celebrity culture with a vitality and truth that
can't be faked.*

Lynn Barver, writing for *The Observer*,
described Vine as *The real deal.*

Literary editor of *The Independent*, Arika Akbar,
compared Vine's examination of the kulture of celebrity

as coming from the same tradition as Pop Art founder.
Stella Vine declared herself a strong connection
to Dracula/Cinderella Andy Warhol,
having studied Drella's work in depth on an art course,
which we wouldn't doubt, not even 4 a sexy sec.

Critic Paul Moody, writing for *The Guardian*,
praised her work for being
*lurid and gutsy paintings causing a storm*
*in the art world,*
and lurid artworks causing a storm in the art world
is the best compliment there is nowadays,
and by far.
*She's causing a fuss. What's wrong with that?,*
sentences Paul at the end of his article.
Nothing's wrong,
Paul,
on the contrary,
as everybody knows.
*And she's in fashion... She's in fashion... Uh, oh...* ♪♪

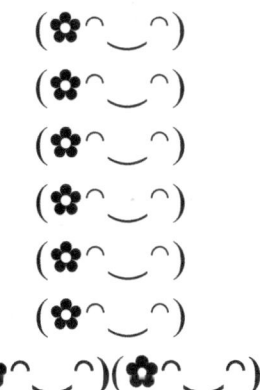

## ART PRICING

(1) Reputation of the artist.
(2) Status of the dealer.
(3) Status of the intended purchaser.
(4) Size of a work.
(5) Opportunism.
(6) Fashion of the artist and/or artwork.
(6) Demand/Supply
(7) Mass production/Scarcity.
(8) Money laundering.
(9) Marketing.
(10) Branding
(11) Speculation.
(12) Media presence (or not).
(13) Novelty (or not).
(14) Prize protection.
(15) Public exhibit.
(16) Auction houses loans.

(...)

(69) ((+_+))

P.S. Collectors give modern artworks as a charity donation so they can avoid paying taxes.

# [[[035]]]

## <u>SPIT</u>

*Everything an artist spits out is art.*
(Kurt Schwitters)

Chinese people spit a lot.
Chinese contemporary art the best there is.
Spit
Spit fire
Spitfire.

Everything can be art if
wholeheartedly/soulfully/intellectually/artistically done.

Rimbaud spitting to a book would be better
than most books.

*This is a call it ain't mine not at all*
*And the world can sit tight and alright*
*Taking your time and get right back online*
*It depends it depends and it comes back again*
*Yes things that everybody would say*
*Believing is hard*
*Spitting is art*
*Things everybody should know*
*The end will come fast*
*Art drinks your heart...* ♪♪

## <u>GOLDEN</u>

*Inter faeces et urinam nascimur.*
(Aurelius Augustinus Hipponensis)

Silence is not golden anymore.
Music is being played all the time everywhere.

Shit is golden
(can't stress it enough.)

# [[[037]]]

*Que no conozca el significado de mi arte
no significa que no lo tenga.*
(Salvador Dalí).

For when you feel lazy.

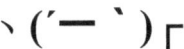

## <u>NEW YORK IS NOAH</u>

*New York Is Now*, by Noah Becker.
Put most of the characters in that
bloodless horror movie
(I'd exclude Lee Ranaldo and the French *monsieur*)
and call it
*NYC: A Confederacy of Douches.*

The masses would love it.
Most people hate contemporary arti$t$.
A huge audience always pays back eventually.

Noah Becker is either the emperor of the douches
or the most funny/ironical/cynical dude in the game.

Impossible to discern if Noah is being 100% himself
or the epitome of what Italian Nobel Prize Winner
Luigi Pirandello
said about the seventh art:
*The film actor feels as if exiled.*
*Exiled not only from the stage but from his own person.*
*With a vague unease, he senses an inexplicable void,*
*stemming from the fact that his body has lost its*
*substance,*
*that he has been volatilized,*
*stripped of his reality, his life, his voice,*

*the noises he makes when moving about,*
*and has been turned into a mute image*
*that flickers for a moment on the screen,*
*then vanishes into silence...*
*The little apparatus will play with his shadow*
*before the audience,*
*and he himself must be content to play*
*before the apparatus.*

( ͡° ͜ʖ ͡°)

## <u>SAFETY NET-ISM</u>

As the critic David Sylvester once famously remarked
of most British contemporary art,
*the rope is only six inches above the safety net,*
so the tightrope for artistic boldness is always
a happy ending stunt.

*Quand être "absolument moderne" est devenu une loi
spéciale proclamée par le tyran,
ce que l'honnête esclave craint plus que tout,
c'est que l'on puisse le soupçonner d'être passéiste.*
(Guy Debord)

When El Greco painted his *sui generis* masterpieces,
in the times of Velázquez, Michelangelo, etc.,
being a vanguardist really, really meant something.
It hasn't mean much since Duchamp's *Fountain*...

Try your worst
Try your best
Try your worst best
Try your best worst
Free as a bird
Untouchable as a ghost.

(^_-)

## FOLLOW YOUR PATH

Jeff Koons and Damien Hirst are the richest
and most famous artists on poppa Earth.
The market needs both walking human brands:

(1) Jeff is the colorful chronicler of the modern world.
Shallow "on purpose", like us.

(2) Damien is the rational *maudit* of the modern world.
"Dark", "deep" and "crazy" on purpose,
like happy *enfant terribles*.

(3) Your original path could be the mix both, and rinse.

(4) Beware the unresolved paradox of the situation:

*Nobody ever listened to me until they didn't know who I
was.*
(Banksy)

*If you want someone to be ignored,
then build a life-size bronze statue of them
and stick it in the middle of town...*
(Banksy)

On the other hand,
we know of artists who made it out of

non-stop self-promotion,
and we suspect that many artists
people don't know *merde* about
would be more famous if people knew who they were
and/or had statues of themselves built.
However, bear in mind that out of stunts
you can get people to be interested on your art
and purchase it…
or just know your name, talk about you,
and never pay attention to your work,
no matter how good…

More food for thought:
Amancio Ortega has always been against marketing
for his multi-billionaire business
and against self-promotion as well,
famously stating that…:
*Uno debería de salir en los periódicos sólo tres veces
en la vida: al nacer, al casarse y al morir.*

┌(; `~,)┐

# [[[041]]]

## <u>ULTIMA CENA</u>

Installation, animation video, canvas...
Whatever looks/works/sells best.

12 last names of Time's *Person of the Year*.

Jesus Christ still in the middle.


丶('― ' ㄨ)／

## LABELS

When labels are the sole manifestation of a work of art,
we are witnessing an exercise in
*Emperor's New Clothes conceptualism.*
Either that or the end of talent and genius at work.

A good one-paragraph label can give you more $$$
than almost any book you could dream writing.
*Credo quia absurdum est.*
Naked, but still an emperor, *madames et monsieurs.*

Check Margaret Honda's installation of her film cases.
A genius excerpt from the label of that installation:
*Margaret Honda's films grow out of a sculptural
practice that privileges a material relationship to the
medium above any narrative or representational
concerns...*
*By displaying them in such a manner, Honda
acknowledges the film's objecthood, giving as much
weight to this quality as to what is projected on-screen.*

On average,
the spectator spends more time reading the label
than looking at the PoMo artwork.
¯\\_(ツ)_/¯

## <u>FAME</u>

*I know you've tried...*
*I know you've cried...*
*I know you've died...*
*A little inside but...*

*Baby, you could be famous... ♩♩*
*You could be the queen of every scene... ♩♩*
*You could be the king of everything... ♩♩*

*Just paint your own blouse... ♩♩*
*Joker around your mouth... ♩♩*
*Blow up this fucking town... ♩♩*

♪ ┌( ・o・)┘ ♪ └( ・o・)┐

*Jean-Michel Basquiat first became famous for his art*
*And then he became famous for being famous*
*And then he became famous for being infamous.*
(Richard Marshall)

¯\_(ツ)_/¯

## JACK & DANIELS

*Considering J&D\* all contemporary art is like
considering R&B\*\* all modern literature.*
Remember those lines for the educated enemies of CA.


But, just between you & me…:
Neu Rach's "Post-surrealism"?
Isn't the best Neu a bad or mediocre Dalí or Magritte?
This doesn't happen with video games, porn,
trap music, action movies and fashion,
contemporary artist…


Photography and graffiti have murdered most painting.
I love not-so-absurd nor cynical yet :D 岳敏君,
but give me, *militaire d'avant-garde*,
Post-Brueghel Chapman brothers' toys
or explosive 蔡国强
any day of the week.


César Aira is too old to know everything, unlike me.


\*Jeff (Koons) & Damien (Hirst)
\*\*Rowling (J. K.) & Brown (Dan)

# [[[045]]]

## FAKE IT 'TIL U FORGET YOU'VE FAKED IT

Poseur > VIP pass > Artist.

The decline of being into having,
and having into merely appearing.

*La première phase de la domination de l'économie
sur la vie sociale avait entraîné dans la définition
de toute réalisation humaine une vidente dégradation
de l'être en avoir.*
*La phase présente de l'occupation totale de la vie
sociale par les résultats accumulés de l'économie
conduit à un glissement généralisé de l'avoir au
paraître, dont tout « avoir » effectif doit tirer son
prestige immédiat et sa fonction dernière.*
*En même temps toute réalité individuelle est devenue
sociale, directement dépendante de la puissance
sociale, façonnée par elle.*
*En ceci seulement qu'elle n'est pas,
il lui est permis d'apparaître.*
(Guy Debord)

( ´ー`)y-~~

## FAKE IT TILL YOU ARE REAL AS FUCK

*Accusing Jeff Koons of hype is like rebuking a fish
for being wet.*
(Robert Hughes)

*Lying becomes superfluous
when the lie has become the truth.*
(Günther Anders)

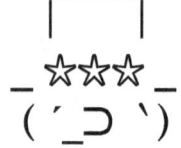

## LIQUID TIMES

We are living in an age of uncertainty, indeed.
Life has never changed this fast.
Fashions have never changed this fast.
Be water in this globalized world,
be water in the internet galaxy,
my friend.
Everything that goes up, comes down
(down, down... ♫♪)
Still wanna be famous? Me too.
So be liquid water, then solid water, then liquid again.
Survival of the (quicker) fittest.

Better to be lucky than good.

*The law is the survival of the fittest...*
*The law is not the survival of the 'better' or 'stronger'.*
*If we give to those words any thing like their ordinary*
*meanings.*
*It is the survival of those which are constitutionally*
*fittest to thrive under the conditions in which they are*
*placed;*
*and very often that which, humanly speaking,*
*is inferiority, causes the survival.*
(Herbert Spencer)

## [[[048]]]

## <u>ACT BEFORE YOU THINK</u>

*Leyendo no se aprende nada,*
*pero se afina la inteligencia, el gusto...*
*pero a quién le interesa refinarse si para tener éxito*
*hay que ser todo lo contrario.*
(César Aira)

*If you love money and you want to be creative,*
*you cannot become creative.*
*The very ambition for money is going to destroy*
*your creativity.*
*If you want fame, then forget about creativity.*
*Fame comes easier if you are destructive.*
(Osho)

It is no mystery that Pablo Picasso's best paintings
were done when he was young and broke
(*Período azul*).
Something similar happened to Salvador Dalí
(1920's-1930's).
Two best painters of the 20th century.
It makes you think.

But how can you be an intellectual, a spiritual being,
a creative man, an artist,
if you are a slave to the money

and then you die?

A poor man cannot understand Hesse's *Siddhartha*.
A hungry man will not read *O livro do desassossego*.
A beggar will not even pay attention to *Las meninas*.
These people who are suffering from hunger don't have
enough energy to make themselves intelligent.
Intelligence comes only when you have superfluous
energy in you.
Your attention spans diminish drastically
when you are thirsty, for example.
The poor are exhausted just in earning for rent & pizza.
They cannot savour nor create masterpieces.
They don't have the time nor peace of mind
only money can buy to do so.

Rimbaud was poor…
but he was taken care of,
while writing most of his works,
by his mother or Paul Verlaine.

Picasso was poor, I said,
and yet to be a poor without needs,
a poor in the sense of carelessness,
he wanted to be rich.
*Quiero ser rico para así vivir tranquilo
como los pobres*, he famously said,
and created many intellectual paintings
hc wouldn't have if he hadn't made it.

*Tú quieres ser pobre sin que te falte nah*
*Yo quiero ser rico pero soy PXXR GVNG.*
(Kaydy Cain)

Only after you achieve what you've always thought
would resolve all of your problems,
and realize firsthand it hasn't,
you can walk the path of spirituality wholeheartedly
and not as a hobby or as something to cross out
of the to-do list
every day,
so respect money and be the worst you can be
to acquire as much as possible
in the shortest amount of time possible,
I recommend.

*There is only one class in the community*
*that thinks more about money than the rich,*
*and that is the poor.*
*The poor can think of nothing else.*
(Oscar Wilde)

John Lennon owned two sport cars at the age of 25
and only afterwards decided to hippy peazy around,
and not completely deluded by the universe
(that *Imagine* song included,
Miss Universe phony song of the century):
*Jay Guru Deva, Ω...*
*Nothing's going to change my world*

*Nothing's going to change my world...* ♪♪
If I had been him I wouldn't have wanted
to even imagine
my world being slightly changed either,
would you?

*Money make ya handsome...* ♪♪

*Waves of joy,*
my friend.

*Be water,*
my comrade.


><γνῶσις>

## <u>WHY SO EXPENSIVE?</u>

Quote Osho, a spiritual playboy:
*I like everything that is beautiful, creative.*
*It contributes to life, it makes life worth living.*
*Only a few people* [like you, contemporary artist]
*have contributed to life's beauty;*
*others are simply a burden on the Earth.*
*Salvador Dalí and Pablo Picasso*
*are our cherished geniuses,*
*so whatsoever price one pays is not enough.*
*It is never enough!*

And artwork can be as expensive
as much as a big shot is willing to pay for it:
no more, no less.

And if the smartarse
Enemy of contemporary art
replies back,
stressing the word "beautiful",
well, then just say that
Dalí's art was wicked and sick
and Picasso's distorted and diabolical,
so we are only following that path of modernity
and if you want traditional beautiful things

you can always purchase costumbrist paintings
on street markets or some charity shops
or, even easier and cheaper,
plastic flowers (which will always look nice :)

## <u>I HAVE HIGH SELF-ESTEEM AND IT'S MAKING ME STARE</u>

A great title taken from a poem of an e-book.

Most movies come from books.

Great artwork titles could easily come from poetry
nobody gives a Chinese yuan for.

Selfies are fashionable.

A statue of a woman with 2 iPhone X for hands
taking pictures of herself,
one pic for each side of her face.
One eye staring at each iPhone,
and huge eyes.


(#^.^#)

## ENERGY DRINK

Mineral water made from woman's tears.

Salty caramel is trendy,
why not slightly salty water?

2 different flavours:

Original
(al punto de sal)

Strawberry
(made with woman's blood [feminist message]).

Patriarchs don't allow men tears nor blood.
It is supposed to be a big shot,
go-doer and/or
player beverage.

It backfires because it is a feminist message
of the actual state of things,
calling for revolt against it,
isn't it?

Σ( ° д °;)

# [[[052]]]

## EMO

The trend of being silly must be reaching its peak.

The trend of being bloody shocking too.

Since human beings keep on falling in and out of love
cry
suffer
and so on
and so on
might be a good idea to go emo
or
PoMoEmo.


R.I.P. Lil Beep.

# [[[053]]]

## 2+2 = 2

Oh, and if the art world tells you 2 is 1,
then 2 is 1, my love, and you should know… ♪♪


●～*

# [[[54]]]

## I WANNA HUG YA

Sculpture.

Man's hands with different scary tools instead of fingers
(a surgical knife, a syringe, etc.)

The arms are penises.

The body is made of two huge hairy balls and
nothing else.

(Feminist message ;)

● ～ *

## <u>SKIN</u>

Traces of skin
in the corner of a gallery.
Different races mixed.
Snake feeling.

Why not?
Remember the 2016 stunt in the
San Francisco Museum of Modern Art
perpetrated by two teenagers,
with one of them leaving his glasses on the floor
and those glasses on the floor being interpreted by
visitors
as bona fide art…

# [[[56]]]

## <u>MADE TO LOVE MAGIC</u>

Bottle of water with highly expensive wine inside.

（＾_＾）o 自自 o（＾_＾）

## <u>SHE'S IN FASHION</u>

Woman dressed in the most ludicrous way possible.

For example:
One sleeper, one high heel, a cravate, an overall…

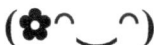

## GENIUS QUOTES

Think of *Masters*
(Louis Vuitton & Jeff Koons).

Same cancer I mean principle.

Quotes from famous authors put on artworks
(canvases, sculptures, installations, whatever works).

~°. .°~

# [[[59]]]

## <u>CAN EXPLAIN</u>

In order to create explanations for your artworks,
check Koons's one about his hoovers.
According to Jeffy,
his *New Hoover Convertibles* are
*displaying themselves in a very kind*
*of classical tradition of art.*
*I mean, you could think of Renaissance sculpture.*
*These are eternal virgins that are being displayed.*

**New Hoover Convertibles, Green, Blue, New Hoover
Convertibles Green, Blue Doubledecker.**
Four vacuum cleaners, acrylic, fluorescent lights
116 x 41 x 28 inches
294.6 x 104.1 x 71.1 cm
© Jeff Koons
1981-1987

## BIG POPPA

Proper religious leader attire.

Jesus's crown of thorns
(not the actual BS super chef one),
a loincloth,
no ring in the finger,
a mirror instead of a crucifix as a necklace,
a torch
(remember Diogenes,
*Diogenes Searching for an Honest Man*,
attributed to Johann Heinrich Wilhelm Tischbein)
et cetera.


**m(_ _)m**

# [[[61]]]

## <u>MY HEART IS AN APPLE</u>

*My hands are of your colour, but I shame to wear a heart so white.*
(Shakespeare)

… Thing is...
capitalism,
technology addiction,
et cetera.

Highbrow Shakespearean title for the artwork.

A childish painting
with white
Apple stickers
on people's chests.

A family portrait.


**m(_ _)m**

## <u>WORK SMART > WORK HARD</u>

Learn how to sell yourself,
branding,
marketing,
how to manipulate the media,
how to manipulate the art market…

Better to be a living meme or walking brand
than a dead poet, isn't it⁇

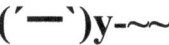

## <u>CUTE BUT ENDANGERED</u>

Cute endangered species painted on big canvases
in a street art manner,
but a colorful one.

Check Rob Pruitt's paintings of pandas
(the ones in the movie *Kingsman: The Secret* Service)

*Everybody loves a panda.*
(Robert P.)

(: Cute political message
[win-win,
in case somebody complains about one or the other] ;)

## <u>BE A CLOWN</u>

*Be a clown, be a clown… ♪♪*
*Everybody loves a clown… ♪♪*

Vomit of Kitsch colorful silliness installation:
a house which walls are covered in confetti rainbows,
cotton candy clouds, doughnut sun, etc.

*Be a clown, be a clown...♪♪*
*All the world loves a clown...♪♪*
*Show 'em tricks, tell 'em jokes*
*And you'll only stop with top folks... ♪♪*

♪ ┌(·o·)┘ ♪ └ ( ·o·) ┐
♪ ┌(·o·)┘ ♪ └ ( ·o·) ┐
♪ ┌(·o·)┘ ♪ └ ( ·o·) ┐
♪ ┌(·o·)┘ ♪ └ ( ·o·) ┐

## WHY CONTEMPORARY ART IS SO BAD?

You should have and answer to that.

Being sincere/honest/real here and there is good
marketing if well used and well timed
(remember Demon Thirst:
*I can't wait to get into a position to make really bad art
and get away with it.
At the moment if I did certain things people would look
at it, consider it and then say "f off".
But after a while you can get away with things.*)

(1)

Because Van Gogh, Modigliani, Hiroshige, etc.,
didn't know *merde*
about motor yachts, 8-star hotels, private jets…

(2)

Because Leonardo da Vinci believed in God,
humankind, civilization, artistic inmortality…
and we cannot believe in any of those anymore.

(3)
Re-read chapter 32.

'Coz it is not meant to be "Good" but "New":
modern, original and shocking.
There are too many crafted, deep and beautiful artworks
from the past already and good artists push boundaries
forward.
The decadent bourgeoise of a 100 years ago
has only got richer and more decadent
(a grasshopper, soiled underpants or a mannequin
rotting by Dalí would not shock anyone today
[just google
"Menstrual blood in contemporary art"]).

*I just wanted to find out where the boundaries were.*
*So far I've found there aren't any.*
*I just wanted to be stopped, and no one will stop me.*
Words of the celebrity Damien H, again.

*Venceréis, pero no convenceréis.*
Sorry, what?
We, contemporary artists, stopped listening after you
said "you'll win", for caviar was coming out of our
ears.

**Homework**:
Read George Orwell's article
*Benefit of clergy: some notes on Salvador Dalí,*
paying special attention to the last paragraphs.

## **WHY NOT?**

99% of contemporary art is built around this question.

There is little you can answer to that.
There is little you cannot get away with.
*Art is what you can get away with* (Andy), indeed.
There is no way to beat that question.

Saint David Foster Wallace wrote
*"Why not?" "Why not?" Why not not, then,*
*if the best reasoning you can contrive is "why not?"*

The contemporary artist answer to DFW is:
What a silly thing to say, sir,
nobody is going to bother answering
such a tongue-twister, dear tortured writer.

Don't be water; be a contemporary artist, my friend.
Why not? Gavin Turk's rubbish bag, rightfully titled
*Bag* ('cause he lives in London and seeing them on the
street from a young age made a huge impact on his life
and psyche and heart and soul and vision of the world)
was awarded the Jack Goldhill Sculpture Prize, by the
Royal Academy of Arts in London.

(´—`)y-~~

## MACHO MAN

Sex sells.
Humour sells.
Machismo sells.
Feminism sells.

1 plop with glans (a "penis")
2 coconuts with pubic hairs attached to
the plop, subsequently attached to
1 man on steroids with
a pair of sunglasses and
1 snobby scarf.

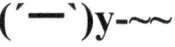

## <u>CHESS</u>

A modern chess set.
Celebrity chess set.
There has never been in the history of humankind
so many celebrities,
due to globalization and modern technologies,
so just pick up your favs.

Besides,
in this our times of meritocracy
being intelligent is no longer a stigma
but a necessity to get a good job and go up the ladder
(as long as you aren't more intelligent
than your university professors, bosses, etc.,
unless you happen to make it out of their system
by being tremendously brilliant and/or lucky enough,
such as in the case of Steve Jobs
[high IQ, hard-worker and, last but not least,
close friends with Steve Wozniak,
in the right moment and in the right place...])


(´─`)y-~~

# [[[69]]]

## <u>FAKE IT TIL IT HURTS</u>

Utterly nonsense disguised as, deep down, sense.

Faux depth.

Remember Jeff Koons'
*Three Ball Total Equilibrium Tank (Two Dr J Silver
Series, Spalding NBA Tip-Off).*

Try this out:
A couple of snails stuck to each other
inside of a display cabinet.
*The end of the world.*

MOSCA enough.

Why not?
Anything goes.

('—`)y-~~

## **<u>MOS = CA</u>**

You can focus on one letter and back it up by bringing
up the words of some great figure of the past.

Today, we'll pick up the vowel *O*,
which stands for *Originality*.

Immanuel Kant considered originality
the essential character of genius:
*Genius is a talent for producing something*
*for which no determinate rule can be given,*
*not a predisposition consisting of a skill*
*for something that can be learned*
*by following some rule or other.*
(Kant)

A modest proposal:
A doughnut cut horizontally in two pieces,
shark jaws between the two parts,
two balls of gold on top as eyes,
and a skeleton body attached to it.
Isn't this original enough?
Many underlying concepts here going on:
*O tempora! O mores!*
*Veritas vos liberabit*
*Memento mori.*

*Tempus fugit.*
*Carpe diem.*
*Plus ultra.*

We just need a title…
The most important part,
along with the explanation,
when it comes to be original for the sake of it…:

**_Tempus edax rerum_**


('─`)y-~~

# [[[71]]]

## MOS = CA

Consonant *M* for me, s'il vous plaît, for *Modern*.
A modern concern... ha!… mmm...
Remember the movie
*Kingsman: The Secret Service.*

A pyramid of humans who crash against
the ceiling of the museum.
Humankind as a virus to the planet.
*Virus* or *Vagina* be the artwork title.

*Aimer son prochain est chose inconcevable.*
*Est-ce qu'on demande à un virus d'aimer un autre*
*virus ?*
(Emil Cioran)

*We are in danger of destroying ourselves by our greed*
*and stupidity.*
*We cannot remain looking inwards at ourselves on a*
*small and increasingly polluted and overcrowded*
*planet.*
(Stephen Hawking)

(´一`)y-~~

## MOS = CA

*S*, for *Sh0ckin'*.
Dalí painted soiled underpants in 1929
(*El juego lúgubre*)
and it infuriated André Breton.
Nowadays it would makes us shrug, if so.


What would shock people nowadays?
What would shock people
after so many tragedies in the last 80 years?
Nazism,
World War II,
Hiroshima,
Chernobyl,
Fukushima,
Stock market crashes…

What shocks people the most nowadays is not
the artwork
but the price the artwork is sold for.

My humble proposal:
A stereotyped feminist woman
dressed in a Green Peace anti-radiation suit

killing a circle of businessmen around her with a katana
(all the heads open, as if somebody had taken a picture
of her in the exact second)
and the sword stuck to the last businessman,
the one who would be farthest away from her.

( ^_^ ) o 自自 o ( ^_^ )

## <u>REVIEW</u>

The problem with most contemporary art is that
it even lacks what it's supposed to embrace.

If Marcel Duchamp created the equation
MOS = CA,
he did so by breaking with all artistic traditions.
However, his followers making a school out of him
fall in the logical inconsequence of following a master
whose art is valuable precisely for
being about not following any tradition or anyone at all.

What are most contemporary art
canvases/installations/sculptures/etc.
but Duchamp's ready-mades
with a bigger size and a better title?
It's all ashes,
hash, a rehash.

If you want to be *der eizinge*,
like Duchamp wanted and became,
you must break with Marcel too
and create your own set of values, taste and
equation.

(´—`)y-~~

## <u>BE MONEY</u>

The best art movement of the 21st century so far
it's the art market itself,
so it deserves a clear artwork
(Hirts's skull is a good metaphor).

Art fairs,
auction houses,
billionaires,
stunts…
what's not to love?

Maybe something
ludicrously obvious:
two statues of Peter Doig:
broke in the 90's
(dressed as an average Joe)
and a multi-millionaire in the 00's
(dressed like Louis XVI).


('—`)y-~~

## <u>RUSHMORE</u>

Mount Rushmore with celebrities instead of presidents.

It's high time for that.

Las Vegas or Asian style.

To be demolished and rebuilt every year.

New york is an unfinished project, isn't it?
Why not a mountain?

Mountains are natural,
so the change it is even more natural
than in an artificial city, so…


(´—`)y-~~

## <u>SEROTONIN</u>

Serotonin alone beats the other 3 famous hormones.

101 idea (u think of another 1 ;):

A fat (no endorphins)
and melancholic (no oxytocin)
billionaire smiling, full of himself.

Money > sex.

If the internet had a way to produce serotonin
as easy as it has one to produce dopamine through porn,
I bet that would be the end of porn's supremacy.

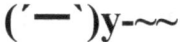

## <u>GENERATION Y</u>

Bees.
Extinction.
Food chain.
End of humanity.

Out of the 100 crop species that provide us
with 90% of our food,
70% are pollinated by bees.

Generation Z coming soon.

The end, internet friend, the end.

Political message.

Still young & beautiful:
Butterflies? Hirst;
Bees? You, my comrade.

Bees in a bowl with milk,
as if they were cheerios,
and a spoon resting against the bowl.


( ^_^ ) o 自自 o ( ^_^ )

## <u>CALIFORNICATION</u>

A skyscraper made of red bricks.
Brutish Americans posing as posh Englishmen.

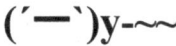

## <u>VIVE LA FRANCE</u>

A gothic cathedral made of aluminium and crystal.
Old France keeping up with hip NY.

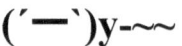

**[[[80]]]**

## FUCK MAMOTHS

A mammoth horn inside of a giant Coca-Cola® bottle.
(getting rusty! Happening!! Sh0CKin'!!!)

Think of 艾未未,
whom painted over vases
from the Neolithic age
Coca-Cola®  signs.


\ | ‾へ‾ | / _ _ _ _ _ _ _ _ θ☆( *o*)/

## <u>PINK MUSIC</u>

An electric guitar made of pink bubblegum.

Why not?
Koons himself has stated that there are no
hidden meanings in his works, nor any critiques.
Act, then think for the interviews.

Jeff Koons's successor.

Gigantic size, needless to say.

New art movement:
K00L Kitsch.

(#^.^#)

# [[[82]]]

## SWEET BACON

Bacon made of:
1) Pink bubblegum.
2) White cream.
3) Condensed milk.

~>°) ~ ~ ~

## <u>CARPE DIEM</u>

Chopsticks made of white chocolate for breakfast,
which is a bowl of rice made of sugar
in a table made of
dark chocolate.

# [[[84]]]

## <u>DIES IRAE</u>

Anti-stress tools to squeeze
in the shape of tits,
penises,
hairy balls,
pussies,
et cetera.


(❀^‿^)

## <u>BEHIND CLOSED DOORS</u>

Installation.

Those murals where you take pictures
by putting your face where a body goes, etc.

The same but with porn scenes.

For men and women.

To touch yourself at home with the image.

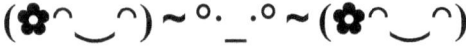

# [[[86]]]

## <u>MARBLE</u>

A room packed with marbles.

Interactive installation.

Walk on them trying not to fall.

*Le génie, c'est l'enfance retrouvée à volonté.*
(Charles Baudelaire)

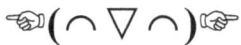

## <u>CHOCO LOCO</u>

Interactive installation.

Melted chocolate.

To enter naked.

Edible.

Rite of passage
(and good for the skin too!).

Chocolate swimming pool in a room.

The room is no more than the swimming pool.

( ^_^ ) o 自自 o ( ^_^ )

## BITTERSWEET DIAMOND

Diamond covered in:
1) Snow
2) Cocaine
3) Salt
4) Sugar.

The icing on the cake would be some drops of jam or blood.

*Al punto de sal.*

● ~ *

## <u>CASTLEVANIA</u>

Installation.

Edible daggers hanging from the ceiling made of sugar with black and grey coloring.

Let go of the past.

Bite 'em.

```
    _γ⌒\_
IXXXXXXXXI
 (  ´m ` )
```

## <u>DESERT</u>

Planet Earth as a pastry.

(1) White cream
(2) Green algae
(3) Blue sugar with coloring.

A nouvelle cuisine dessert.

Political message.
Plain and reductive.
Bansky style
*because his work looks dazzingly clever to idiots*
(Charlie Brooker).


● ~ *

## TVOOK

A television in the shape of a book.

Façade for Americans.

*Television is an excellent system*
*when one has nothing to lose,*
*as in the case with a nomadic and rootless country*
*like the United States,*
*but in Europe the affect of television is that of a*
*bulldozer*
*which reduces culture*
*to the lowest possible denominator.*
(Marc Fumaroli)

( ^_^ ) o 自自 o ( ^_^ )

## <u>ARE YOU A DOG OR A CAT PERSON?</u>

Fur coats made of cats and dogs.

Yoko Ono is wearing one mixing both.

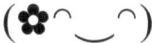

# [[[93]]]

## **POST-HIRSTURK**

An open shark full of shit inside
(plastic bags, bottles, etc.)

Damien Hirst's and Gavin Turk's influence.

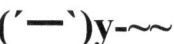

# [[[94]]]

## <u>HARMACY</u>

A pharmacy full of both legal and illegal drugs.

America's opioid crisis.

Post-Hirst.

(´—`)y-~~

## <u>VULTURE KULTURE</u>

Doughnut > tuber.

Destroy masterpieces.

One from each country.

Remember Duchamp's moustache on La Gioconda
and Woody Allen's book *Getting Even*.

Bother the pedants.

True intellectuals know those masterpieces
don't deserve a better destiny in our current world.


(´ー`)y-~~

# [[[96]]]

## <u>TAINTED LUST</u>

Perfume.

100% women's tears.

It will attract 'em all, bro.

('一`)y-~~

## <u>TAINTED LUV</u>

Perfume.

100% man's sweat.

It will attract 'em all, It grrl.

('ー`)y-~~

## <u>PINK POWER</u>

Nuclear power plant made of cotton candy.

Fear of nuclear weapons nowadays.

Political & environmental message.

Habit makes everything bearable.

Everything is open to humour
after some time has passed.

We live within technology.

We cannot go back.

We can only make the best use of it.

We are living in a bear trap.

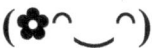

# [[[99]]]

## <u>CRYBABY</u>

A golden necklace *al punto de caramelo*.

Lick it here and there
in order to remember to be thankful for what you got
and overcome mental conditioning
of always wanting what you don't have
and thinking the grass is greener on another ride.

><>

## **CRYBABY 2**

Diamond ring with adjustable sparkling light.
*Quiero dar a entender que debería producir destellos*
*cada cierto tiempo*, got it, sir?
Like every 30 minutes or something.

Same principle as in *Crybaby*.

## NEXTMODERNISM

Empty books as a statement of the state of culture.

*In the old days,*
*books had awful covers yet*
*marvelous content;*
*nowadays,*
*it is the other way around.*
(Giacomo Leopardi).

*Sì,* Leopardi said that in the early 19th century!
Just picture him in Barnes & Noble today!!

They can be seen in cafés, Ikea,
upper middle flats with lovely sea views...
as decoration.
There are even wall stickers with the picture of a shelf...

*We should remember that all the arts are fine arts*
*and all the arts decorative arts.*
(Oscar Wilde)

White canvases with the plastic on them and all,
just signed on top quickly
or spited with vomit or juice in the mouth
or some colorful liquid you happen to be drinking.

# NeXTmodernism.

*People often talk as if there was an opposition between
what is beautiful and what is useful.
There is no opposition to beauty except ugliness:
all things are either beautiful or ugly,
and utility will be always on the side of
the beautiful thing,
because beautiful decoration is always on the side of
the beautiful thing,
because beautiful decoration is always an expression of
the use you put a thing to and the value placed on it.*
(Oscar Wilde)

キタ━━( ゜∀ ゜)━━━!!!!!

## <u>LIFE ON MARS</u>

Planet Mars with the Hollywood sign on it.

The land where life comes plausible.

We don't have a lot of time left to fuck around on Earth.

( ^_^ ) o 自自 o ( ^_^ )

## INFLATABLE

A futuristic child's inflatable swimming pool
with weird toys due to nuclear waste:
fishes with 3 eyes (*The Simpsons* style),
horses with 3 legs (back leg in the middle of its body),
figures which look like Dalí's painting
*Premonición de la Guerra Civil*
and other aberrations for you to come up with.


('一`)y-~~

# [[[104]]]

## **ACTION MEN & HOT BARBIES**

A fish tank full of
Rambo men,
smokin' hot barbies
and little cute objects for typical aquariums.

Highly evolved.

K00L Kitsch.

Check Hidetomo Kimura's *Aquarium*.

R.I.P., 天野尚.


('一`)y-~~

# [[[105]]]

## HI, HOW ARE YOU

6 birds trapped in a six-pack ring.

To be put at the entrance of the gallery.

><(((*>

# [[[106]]]

## <u>THE INFINITE JEST</u>

A statue made of only mouths LOOLING around.

*Cracked smiles… Silent shouts…* ♪♪

# [[[107]]]

## <u>LAST LIVING SOUL</u>

Environmental art.
Installation art.
Fantasy of being the last living soul on Earth.
*Walking Dead* feeling.
Abandoned Detroit church feeling.
Abandoned shopping mall feeling.


(´—`)y-~~

## HALLELUJAH

Norman Rockwell's *Saying Grace*:
sold for $46 million (including a buyer's premium)
at Sotheby's in December 2013,
setting a new record price for Rockwell's art.

Rockwell was paid $3.500 in 1951
(equivalent to $32.294 in 2016).
It was the cover of a magazine
(*The Saturday Evening Post*).

First time I saw it,
I thought it was a costumbrist Camel's advert,
what about you?

Learn from my mistake!
Watch out!!
*¡¡¡Al loro, que es de oro!!!*

The contemporary art market
is like chess
is like love
is like seduction
is like poetry is like art
(so nuanced that it can drive you mad).

## <u>O TEMPORA! O MORES!</u>

If you take religion and afterlife out of the equation,
you still have great art,
not as great as Dante's or Leonardo's,
but a huge amount of masterpieces
still in the 19th century
and even in the 20th century.

If you take artistic immortality out of the equation,
due to nuclear weapons and the internet galaxy
(who would have found self-published books,
such as Lautréamont's *Chants*,
on CreateSpace?
The web is a little bit bigger than Paris...)
you get what the world around you deserves,
which is contemporary art.

Be an artist of your own time.

(´—`)y-~~

## EL ÁNGEL REVITALIZADOR

Video/installation/happening/whatever.
3 gorgeous black skyscrapers
with Christmas lights on them working 24/7,
some shops and parks for the kids around
(and a school
and a Noah's Ark
for the adults to work so
vain existence can never exist,
for *unless the Lord builds the house,*
*the builders labor in vain* (Psalm 127),
and the rest would be cold driven snow.

If the faith is unchanged and rock solid,
then the gates of Hades never prevailed in the end.

An experiment on the human condition.
Watch *El ángel exterminador,* by Luis Buñuel.
*Dogville* feeling.

*Noël sur la terre !*
(in its isolated beauty it feels like post-apocalyptical)

We see the skyscrapers from a distance,
us hiding behind a snow lump.

# [[[111]]]

## <u>TRUMP KOREA</u>

Donald Trump.
North Korea.

*President Trump Becomes a Wonder Woman,*
*Unifies the Country and Fights Rocket Man*
by American artist Peter Saul.

Now it's high time for an apocalyptical canvas.


● ~ *

## THE VOID

Robert Ryman's
*Bridge*
was sold for $20.6 million
at a Christie's auction in 2015.

I personally prefer *The Bridge*,
by Swedish band The Knife.

20th century rootless American minimalist painter
selling for more than the genius of Salvador Dalí...
Andy Warhol sells for more than Picasso too, so…
American's biggest talent is to make money,
which is rarer than artistic talent, after all.
RE$P€CT.

But the Frenchmen,
*oh là là*,
always the Frenchmen first
(Courbert, Duchamp, Blek le Rat…):
Alphonse Allais,
*Première communion de jeunes filles chlorotiques par*
*un temps de neige,*
from 1883!
Modern, Original and Shocking.
With a great title.

Intelligent concept.
Proto-minimalist or even post-minimalist.
(and Dada, Neo-Dada &/or Fluxus…)

There's no need for another white monochrome
painting
after that one.
Everything after that lacks what makes
contemporary art interesting:
Modernity,
Originality…

Ha!
Here's the deal:
*Bridge* is still ShOCKingggg,
for
whenever you are able to sell an artwork at a high price,
no matter which one,
the shocking value will persist and even increase
('cause it will bother the working and middle class),
the absurder the higher,
hence why contemporary art will never die.

It's artistically valuable,
though,
out of
nostalgia
&
generational marketing:

a minimalist artist's artwork
when Minimalism was at its peak
(no matter that Russians and Frenchmen
had done that it half a century before or more)
followed by many as a reaction to
emotional Abstract expressionism.


● ~ *

## MARCEL DUCHAMP CHAMP!

*I force myself to contradict myself in order to avoid conforming to my own taste.*

*The creative act is not performed by the artist alone; the spectator brings the work in contact with the external world by deciphering and interpreting its inner qualifications and thus adds his contribution to the creative act.*

*Destruction is also creation.*

*Art is either plagiarism or revolution.*

*What I have in mind is that art may be bad, good or indifferent, but, whatever adjective is used, we must call it art, and bad art is still art in the same way that a bad emotion is still an emotion.*

*Art is not about itself but the attention we bring to it.*

*My idea was to chose an object that wouldn't attract me, either by its beauty or by its ugliness. To find a point of indifference in my looking at it, you see.*

## <u>MORE MARCEL'S QUOTES</u>

*Let us consider two important factors, the two poles of
the creation of art: the artist on the one hand, and on
the other the spectator who later becomes the posterity.
To all appearances, the artist acts like a mediumistic
being who, from the labyrinth beyond time and space,
seeks his way out to a clearing.*
*If we give the attributes of a medium to the artist, we
must then deny him the state of consciousness on the
esthetic plane about what he is doing or why he is
doing it. All his decisions in the artistic execution of the
work rest with pure intuition and cannot be translated
into a self-analysis, spoken or written, or even thought
out.*

*The most interesting thing about artists is how they live.*

*Not everyone is an artist but everyone is a fucking
critic.*

*There is no solution because there is no problem.*

*Art has the lovely  habit of ruining all artistic theories.*
**(´ー`)y-~~**

## ANY FIN GO-GO

If driving sport cars you like,
if Michelin restaurants you like,
if big yachts you like,
if private jets you like,
why, nobody will oppose.

When spot paintings are being sold for millions
like hot dogs made of Satan's blood…
anything goes.

The world has gone mad today…
and good's bad today
and black's white today
and day's night today
and that gent today
you gave a cent today
once had several chateaux.

When a vomit on a canvas can be sold,
when cleaning ladies are mistaking artworks
for rubbish all around the globe,
well, then you undoubtedly know… that...
we rock.
¯\_(ツ)_/¯

... and so we reached, on the verge of giving up, the end of our comedy. Like you, I would like to go back to the jacuzzi in my favourite brothel now, but before that I'd like to apologize to those who wanted more and those who wanted less. Those who got what they came for... deserve it.

P.S. By the time you read this book it might probably be wfjasbfjkashfi*LY* outdated, as well as your favourite song from 2020, so I apologize 4 dat 2, if so.

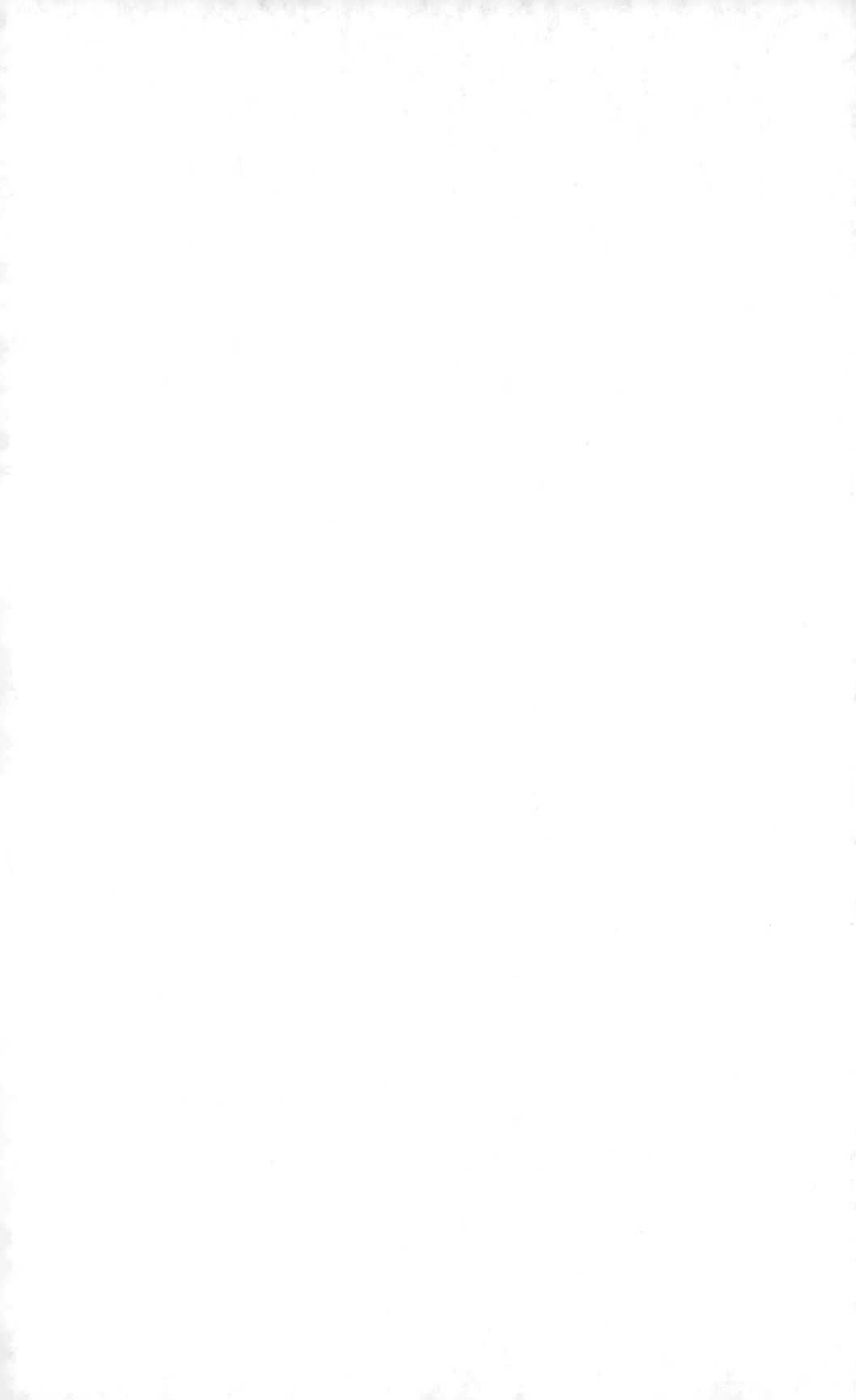